W9-ALM-504

The Wonder of
BATS

ANIMAL WONDERS

ANIMAL WONDERS

ANIMAL WONDERS

ANIMAL WONDERS

ANIMAL WONDERS

• ANIMAL WONDERS • ANIMAL WONDERS •

To my children, Cindy, Kate, and Nathan. Thank you for showing me the wonders of our world as seen through the curious eyes of a child. And to my husband, Wayne, for his support.

— Kathryn T. Lundberg

For a free color catalog describing Gareth Stevens Publishing's list of high-quality books and multimedia programs, call 1-800-542-2595 (USA) or 1-800-461-9120 (Canada). Gareth Stevens Publishing's Fax: (414) 332-3567.

Library of Congress Cataloging-in-Publication Data available upon request from publisher. Fax: (414) 332-3567 for the attention of the Publishing Records Department.

ISBN 0-8368-2660-4

First published in North America in 2000 by
Gareth Stevens Publishing
A World Almanac Education Group Company
330 West Olive Street, Suite 100
Milwaukee, WI 53212 USA

This edition is based on the book *Bats for Kids* © 1996 by Kathryn T. Lundberg, with illustrations by John F. McGee, first published in the United States in 1996 by NorthWord Press, Inc., Minocqua, Wisconsin, and published as *Bat Magic for Kids* in a library edition by Gareth Stevens, Inc., in 1996. All photographs © 1996 by Merlin D. Tuttle, Bat Conservation International. Additional end matter © 2000 by Gareth Stevens, Inc.

Printed in the United States of America

1 2 3 4 5 6 7 8 9 04 03 02 01 00

The Wonder of
BATS

by Amy Bauman and Kathryn T. Lundberg
Photographs by Merlin D. Tuttle
Illustrations by John F. McGee

Gareth Stevens Publishing
A WORLD ALMANAC EDUCATION GROUP COMPANY

On warm summer evenings, the air fills with life. Lightning bugs twinkle, and crickets chirp.

Dark creatures dart back and forth through the night — bats!

Bats are the
only true flying
mammals. They
fly the night skies
all over the world,
except in the
coldest places.
There are more
than 980 kinds,
or species, of bats.
Bats make up
one-fourth of all
mammal species.

free-tailed bats

bumblebee bat

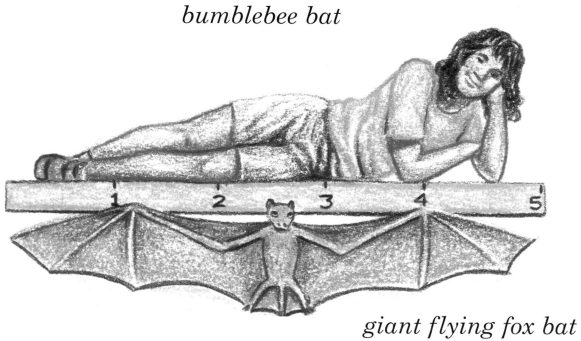

giant flying fox bat

8

The bumblebee bat is tiny.
Its wingspan is only 5 inches
(13 centimeters). Western
pipistrelle bats are the
smallest in the United States.

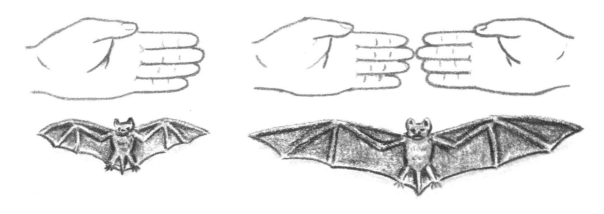

*bumblebee bat: 5-inch
(13-cm) wingspan*

*western pipistrelle bat:
9-inch (23-cm) wingspan*

Giant flying fox bats have a
5-foot (1.5-meter) wingspan!

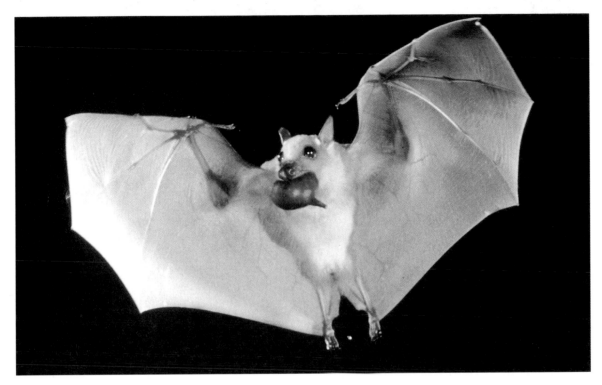

fruit bat

Different species of bats look different from each other. Ears, eyes, noses, and faces can be big, small, wrinkly, or smooth.

wrinkle-faced bat

Bats often live together and roost in groups called colonies. During the day, bats sleep. At night, they fly off to search for food.

The little brown bat is common in North America. This bat is brown and furry and has a 10-inch (25-cm) wingspan. It weighs less than 1/2 ounce (14 grams).

In winter, little brown bats hibernate in dark, quiet places, such as caves. Caves are moist inside, and temperatures stay cool — just the way the bats like it.

little brown bats

Mexican free-tailed bats on next page

Bats roost in everything from caves to barns to bamboo stems. Honduran white bats roost in tents they make out of plants.

Honduran white bats

To make the tents, the bats
bite the leaves and then fold
them along the bite lines.

Bats swoop and dart through the night to hunt for food — often insects. When bats look for food, most of them do not use their eyes.

Instead, bats use their ears to find things. This is called echolocation.

leaf-nosed bat

During echolocation, a bat makes a clicking sound as it flies. The sound strikes an object and echoes back to the bat's large ears.

A fisherman bat swoops down,

From the echo, the bat can tell what the object is and where the object is located — even in the dark!

grabs its prey, and flies off (on next page).

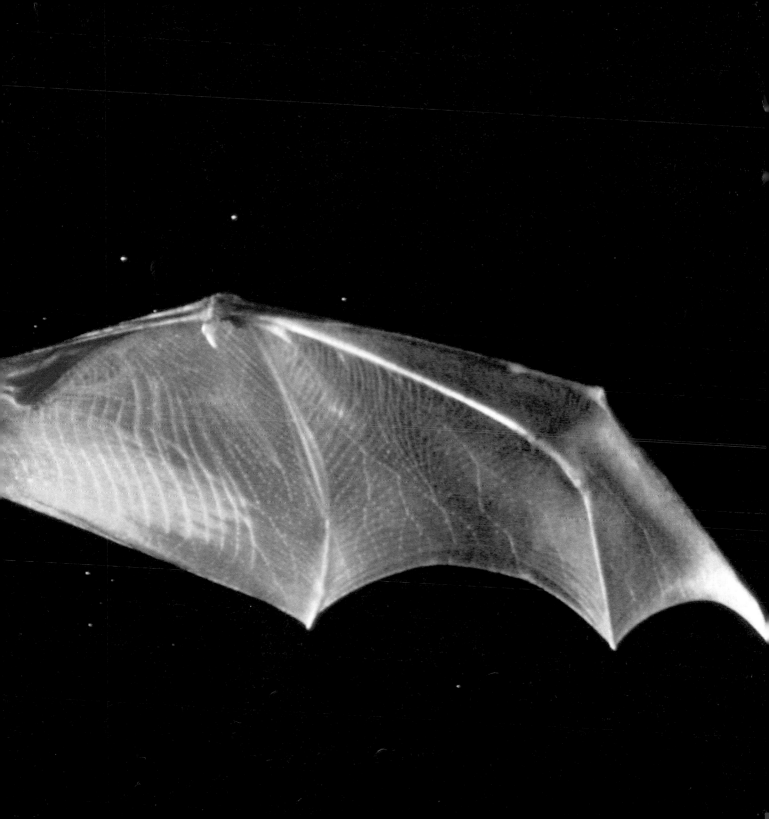

All bats can see,
hear, and smell.
Not all bats can
use echolocation,
though. Some
bats, like the fruit
bat, depend on
night vision and
a strong sense of
smell. Each night,
these bats follow
the sweet smell of
ripe fruit to find
their dinner.

fruit bat

Scientists often go into caves to collect bats and study them. They measure things like wingspan and weight. Then they let the bats go. Some scientists use special detectors that can record the high-pitched sounds bats make.

Scientists collect bats for study.

Bat wings are covered with fur. The wings are actually arms with very long fingers. A stretchy skin covers each arm and hand. This design allows bats to fly quickly. Some bats fly as fast as 65 miles (105 kilometers) an hour!

Bats' feeding habits play an important role in nature. Each night, one little brown bat can eat more than its weight in insects. Fruit-eating bats scatter fruit seeds through their droppings, and new plants grow.

heart-nosed bat

Nectar-drinking bats pollinate plants like bees do. The Egyptian fruit bat pollinates the African baobab tree. This tree provides food and shelter for many animals.

long-nosed bat

Some bats eat meatier meals.
Fisherman bats use their
long legs, big feet, and sharp
claws to catch fish. Tropical
frog-eating bats eat — you
guessed it — frogs!

frog-eating bat

vampire bat

Vampire bats live in Central and South America. They drink blood from animals such as cows, sheep, and horses, as the animals sleep. The animals don't even feel the bites.

Bats also provide a useful resource. People use bat droppings, called guano, as fertilizer. The smelly guano "mined" from bat caves can be harmful for people to breathe.

A mask helps this photographer breathe safely.

In early spring, female bats have babies, or pups. The females form a colony just for mothers and babies. Usually, each female gives birth to only one pup at a time.

QUIET!
NURSERY

Pups stay in the colony while mothers hunt for food. When a mother returns, she finds her baby again by following its call. Bat babies, like other mammals, drink their mothers' milk. They grow quickly and soon learn to fly and hunt for themselves.

fruit bats

A bat can live thirty years — *if* it isn't eaten by another predator, such as an owl. Like bats, owls search for meals at night.

little brown bat

All over the world, owls and other birds of prey feed on bats. Snakes eat bats, too. Bats will sometimes even eat other bats!

Other animals are only a small threat to bats. Humans can be much more threatening. Some people are afraid of bats and destroy them or their homes.

flying fox bats

long-nosed bats

The pesticides people use can hurt insect-eating bats. Logging and building projects destroy bat habitats.

We must do our best to protect bats and their homes. They are a unique and valuable part of our world.

Glossary

echolocation – the way some animals use sound waves to locate objects

fertilizer – a substance that enriches the soil

habitats – the places where animals and plants live in nature

hibernate – to spend a long period of time in a resting, sleeplike state

mammals – animals with hair or fur that feed their young with mother's milk

pollinate – to move pollen from male to female parts of flowers for fertilization

predator – an animal that hunts other animals for food

roost – to rest or sleep

species – a group of animals or plants with similar characteristics

wingspan – the length of an animal's wings from one tip to the other

Index